MW00807116

A Place Far Away

By Amaya and Angela Allen

Illustrated by violeta samson

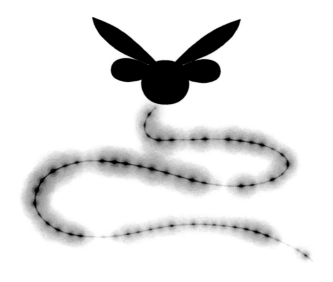

Copyright © 2016 Amaya and Angela Allen
All rights reserved. This book or parts thereof may not be reproduced in any
form, stored in any retrieval system, or transmitted in any form by any means—
electronic, mechanical, photocopy, recording, or otherwise—without prior written
permission of the publisher, except as provided by United States of America
copyright law. For permission requests, write to the publisher, at "Attention:
Permissions Coordinator," at the address below.

Masterful Publishing
PO Box 6248
McKinney, Texas 75070
angela@masterfulcollective.com

To all widows, From Angela
I grieve with you. I hope this book helps to heal some wounds your children will face about death. God promised to heal broken hearts, believe it!

To my hero, Love Amaya
I know you are standing by the tree of life in heaven eating right now. I miss you. I love you to heaven and back.

To my grandparents (rest in heaven with your son Nana), Love Amaya
I just want to say you have been such an encouragement and inspiration to me. Thank you for being there for me and helping my mom raise me and for teaching me how to be a better person. I love you!

To Ms. Suzan and the Taylor Dance Center dance teachers, Love Amaya
Thank you for helping me dance like nobody's watching. Thank you for supporting my love of dance and thank you for opening up so many opportunities for me.

So many people! There were so many people out there, waiting to see her ballet class dance their final recital. Mackayla peeped out at all those faces. Mama should be there, and Grandpa. Daddy was supposed to come home from the hospital today. Maybe, just maybe he'd be well enough to come, too. Seeing her dance always made him smile.

All of a sudden, she didn't feel like dancing. She felt like throwing up.

"Come on!" whispered her friend Sierra. "You know the routine backwards." Mackayla swallowed and shook her head.

"Just put your shoes on," Sierra said. "You can do anything in those ballet shoes." She was right!

When Mama came to the changing room, Mackayla ran to hug her.

"Did you see my jeté, Mama? It was the best I ever did!"

Something was wrong. Mama was crying.

Mama never cried.

Her hands went cold. She felt like throwing up again. "What's the matter, Mama? Didn't they let Daddy come home today?"

"Oh, honey." Mama held her so tight she couldn't breathe. "Daddy's not coming home. Oh, Baby, Daddy's gone to Heaven."

Mama's kisses left wet tears in Mackayla's hair. "It might be a long time, but we will see him again. Then we'll be together forever."

The whole world spun. She felt herself falling. Down, down, in a deep hole. She screamed. When you have a nightmare about falling, and you scream, then you wake up. But she couldn't wake up, because it was real.

So many people! There were so many people at the house, and the church, and the cemetery. They all wanted to hug Mackayla, and say dumb things that didn't help at all.

When she could finally get away, she ran to her room and locked the door. One thing she had to do right away those ballet shoes went straight in the trash.

She got her best drawing pad and her favorite colors. Nobody knew about her secret spot, so nobody could find her. Good. She closed her eyes and made a wish. She wished she could see her father again. She wished so hard, a big fat tear squeezed out of her eye and dripped onto the picture.

Mackayla opened her eyes and gasped. She turned off her flashlight, but it was no trick. The sun was glowing by itself. It rose up slowly from the paper, a tiny dot like a lightning bug. It zipped around her head so fast, she got dizzy.

What if it got loose? She jumped up and caught it in her book, slamming it shut, tight.

She hid the book under her bed. Nobody could know about this. No way.

When Grandpa took her out to the lake, Mackayla watched the clouds moving across the water. You could see the trees upside-down in the lake. She was upside-down, too.

"I'm so sorry I missed your recital, sweetheart," Grandpa said. "I'll be there for the next one."

She shook her head. "I quit ballet."

Grandpa touched her cheek. His hand was wrinkly and scratchy, but so warm. "How are you doing, Baby?"

Mackayla pointed at her upside-down self. A water-bug skated across her reflection, breaking it up in ripples that scattered her face in a hundred directions. "I feel like that."

Grandpa nodded. "Honey, your Mama loves you, and I love you, and Jesus loves you." He put his arm around her. "Sometimes Jesus takes us through hard places, and all you can do is follow. His love will always stay with you and guide you."

"Here."

From his pocket he pulled a dainty, shining chain. "Your Daddy got this for your next birthday, but I think you should have it now."

The little charm bracelet sparkled in the sunshine.

That afternoon, Mackayla pulled her ballet shoes out of the trash.

"I'm brave," she said, and put them on. "I can do anything."

She found her drawing pad. She took a deep breath. "Follow the love," she said.

She opened the book. Out came the little light, quick as a dragonfly. It circled around the room, one…two…three times.

"Oh," she breathed. The light was so bright, so beautiful, like a spark shooting up from a campfire in the night.

Zoom! It was gone down the stairs.

"Wait for me, Sparkie!"

Mackayla ran to keep up. "Where are you going, Sparkie?"

It went straight into the woods. She loved the woods, especially on a hot day like this, when the leaves made cool shade and the birds whistled high above her.

Sparkie led her between the trees…and around the trees…and even over some trees!

Finally, they came to a huge old trunk with a hole in the middle, and the lightning bug flew inside the tree.

"Come back, Sparkie!" She called. "I can't fit in there."

But it turned out she could. And when she wriggled through…

She shivered. "Where are we, Sparkie?"

She couldn't hear the birds now, just rustling leaves and creaking twigs. Far away, a deep moan made her shiver again. She stared at the little light so hard her eyes watered. "Don't you leave me, Sparkie," she said.

She followed it deeper into the forest.

A whack from behind knocked the breath right out of her!

The dog's bark was loud as a roar, so close Mackayla could feel his hot breath on her face. She screamed.

She screamed so loud and high that the dog jumped back and pawed at his ears.

Her face got hot. "Bad dog! I never did anything to you. Go home! Bad dog!"

The dog tucked his tail and hung his head.

The little light circled around the dog.

"Don't you have a home?" asked Mackayla.

The dog whimpered.

She put her hand out carefully, the way her father taught her to. The dog licked it.

"You want to be friends?" she asked.

Sparkie zoomed around the dog until Mackayla saw the glint on his collar. -- A gold lion.

"Is that your name? Leo?"

The dog gave a happy bark. She put the lion on her charm bracelet. Sparkie flew on into the forest.

"Come on, Leo," she said. Soon the ground changed. It got hard to climb.

Then it got hard to see. Leo could jump from rock to rock. He pranced ahead. Mackayla couldn't catch her breath. "Not so fast, Sparkie!"

When she reached the top, she heard a yelp. Then another came from far ahead, high and helpless. "Leo!" She scrambled down.

"Leo! I'm coming!" Mackayla ran to help him, but Sparkie flew right into her face. She stopped just in time -- one foot came down, squelch!

She looked around for a solid place. "Hang on, Leo. I'll get you out." She reached as far as she could. "Come on, Leo. Give me your paw. Shake! Shake hands!"

Just a bit farther…

Oh, no! Her splash pushed Leo even farther away. He was up to his ears now, paddling hard. Then up to his nose. Then he sank out of sight.

"Oh, Leo, no!" She reached for him, but the mud pulled her lower and lower.

She cried. She cried because she was scared, and cold, and tired, and she wanted to go home. She cried for Leo, and her Mama, and her Daddy, and herself.

She cried so much it made a puddle. The puddle grew to a pond, and the pond grew to a flood. The flood carried her up and up, out of the bog, out of that valley.

When the wave broke and rolled back, she was on dry ground.

"Leo!" She hugged him till they both smelled like wet dog, and she didn't even care. He licked her face.

A breeze ruffled Leo's fur, and Mackayla shivered. She hugged him harder to keep warm.

The wind grew stronger, and they huddled down in the dry leaves. The wind blew away all the flood-water, till nothing was left but one perfect crystal of salt. Sparkie circled around them while Mackayla hung the crystal on her bracelet.

"One from Daddy. One from you. One from the water and the wind." Mackayla snuggled against Leo's warm back. "I wonder where the next one will come from?" Sparkie zipped away, then back, urging Mackayla to get up and move on. "But I'm so tired," she said. "Can't we just rest a minute?"

Crash!

Mackayla jumped up. "What was that?"

Leo whined and crept backward, his ears flat on his head.

Crash!

Whatever it was, it was big, and it was getting closer.

Mackayla pressed back against a big rock. A growl sent shivers down her neck. She couldn't run. She couldn't move. She couldn't breathe.

Out of the shadows, a Beast leaped. Mackayla jumped away, but not quick enough. The Beast caught her feet in its enormous jaws and shook her.

Mackayla screamed and fought, but the Beast held tight. Its snarl ran right through her bones.

Leo grabbed her by the collar. For one awful moment, Mackayla thought she might get pulled in half.

Snap! Leo yanked her right out of her ballet shoes. With a slurp and a slobber, the Beast chomped them up. Mackayla ran into the dark.

She stumbled. She glanced back.

The Beast crashed through the trees. Mackayla gasped.

The Beast was getting bigger.

Leo pushed her up, and she ran on. She dodged between two trees and stopped -- There was nowhere else to run. "Sparkie, help!" Mackayla cried. Sparkie darted in front of her, glowing. There! A crack - so small. Could she fit? She had to. Mackayla slipped inside, just as the Beast crashed into the rock. Its horrible claws scratched at the opening, but the Beast couldn't reach her. Leo whimpered. "Leo!" She hugged him. "Where's Sparkie?" Over her head, the little light glowed softly. "You saved me -- both of you. Thank you." Mackayla laid her head on Leo's soft neck. "Thank you for being my friends."

Sparkie flew a triple loop-the-loop and buzzed toward the crack. The Beast's paw clattered on the rock. Mackayla rubbed her eyes and looked again. It was smaller. Mackayla had an idea. She scratched Leo under the chin. "You know, Leo, Grandpa said that Love would guide me. Looks like he's right."

It worked! The Beast's paw got even smaller. Mackayla clasped Leo's furry face in both hands and whispered, "Listen up, Leo. I've got a plan." Leo burst out of the cave, barking his angriest bark. The Beast dodged away from his sharp teeth.

Mackayla jumped out. The Beast raised its claws, but Mackayla clenched her fists, took a deep breath and shouted: "My Daddy taught me to stand up for myself, and I can stand up to you!" The Beast's eyes got wide. It shrunk a whole foot, like a balloon with the air let out.

Leo ran to Mackayla's side and snarled at the Beast. Mackayla yelled, "My Daddy told me I'm a child after God's own heart." She pointed her finger at the Beast. "That means you're not the boss of me!"

The Beast waved its paws in the air and tried to roar, but it was no bigger than Mackayla herself now. Its voice sounded like a tired old goat.

Mackayla stood tall, her hands on her hips. "My Daddy told me he'd love me forever. I can feel it in my heart, and I always will."

Where did it go?

Mackayla brushed away the fallen leaves to find all that was left of the Beast.

Mackayla hung the charm on her bracelet.

Wow! She moved her arm, and the light moved with it. "Leo, look!" The gnarled old trees showed their graceful branches. Dew glimmered on leaves. A movement caught her eye. A shadow. A person? Mackayla moved the light again.

"Daddy!" Mackayla ran to him.

Her father hugged her so tight, she lost her breath. "Daddy, how did you get here?"

His voice rumbled against her cheek. "I've been with you the whole time, sweetheart. You just couldn't see me."

Mackayla pulled her father by the hand, and Sparkie led the way.

Mackayla danced and chattered as she told her father all her adventures. Even Leo pranced and jumped. His bark sounded like laughter.

Mackayla's father smiled. "I love to watch you dance, Baby. Don't ever stop dancing."

Sparkie circled around them. Mackayla's father knelt down and hugged her. "You be good to your Mama. Study hard in school. I'm so proud of you, Mackayla."

"Wait..." Mackayla grabbed her father's neck. This sounded like goodbye.

She looked around. The giant tree with the hole stood right in front of her. "This is goodbye, honey. I can't come back with you." Her father kissed her. "You know I love you forever."

"No, Daddy, no!" Mackayla's eyes got hot and prickly. A big glob of awfulness clogged up her throat. "I don't want to leave you. I can't lose you again."Her father squeezed her hand. "Honey, you have a whole life waiting for you.

I want you to grow up and be happy."

"How can I be happy? I'd have to forget you."

Mackayla sobbed. "Oh, Daddy, I don't want to forget you." Something yanked Mackayla's arm down, hard. "Stop it, Leo!" But it wasn't Leo. The light went out.

"Daddy!" Mackayla screamed. The chain on Mackayla's wrist dragged her up and up. She kicked and fought, but she couldn't get loose. She reached for the clasp, but the chain dug into her skin. She couldn't undo it.

Flash!

Sparkie zoomed past her, his light so bright it hurt her eyes. One giant loop, and Sparkie smashed into the chain link. It broke with a jerk, and Mackayla fell. The Beast snapped its jaws. Sparkie zipped back and forth, but --

Snap!

Sparkie was gone.

Mackayla screamed as she fell. Down, down, right through the hole in the tree. The falling seemed like it went on forever.High above, the Beast roared and grew even bigger.

But something was different.

Something glowed from deep inside it.

With a dreadful ripping noise, beams of light split through the Beast's fur.

Thunder shook the air. The flash was so bright, Mackayla covered her eyes. The Beast was gone.

For just a second, in the flash, she thought she saw her father. Mackayla opened her eyes. How did she get home? Everything looked normal, until she saw the little charm bracelet on her nightstand. She grabbed it and counted the charms.

Ballet shoes.
A lion.
A crystal.
A flower.
And one more -- a firefly.

Mackayla put her bracelet on, but nothing magical happened. Or so she thought, till she looked in the mirror. She was smiling.
"Together forever…for real," she whispered. She looked out the window toward the woods. The sun was just beginning to turn the dewdrops silver. Far away, she heard a dog barking. It was a happy bark, that sounded almost like a laugh.

THE END.

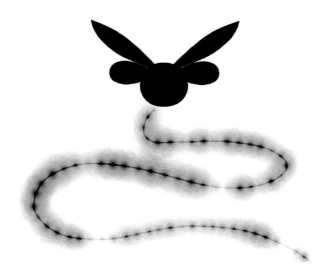

Since you have been gone, I have been feeling?

Draw a picture

Share a favorite memory

Draw a picture

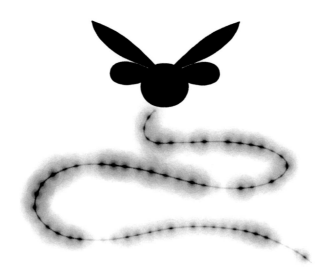

Share something you and your family do now

Draw a picture of your family

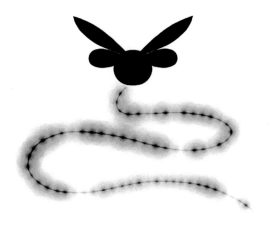

Goodbye Letter to your loved one

Dear   ,

I am sad to say goodbye because

I will always remember what you taught me about

We remember you by

I love spending time with you by

Thank you for being my

I will always love you.

54290983R00026

Made in the USA
San Bernardino, CA
12 October 2017